THIS IS WHAT FREEDOM LOOKS LIKE

KENNEDY KREZI OKUMU

D1453871

THIS IS WHAT FREEDOM LOOKS LIKE
Published by Krezi Glogal Management, LLC, Evans, Colorado, USA

First edition

This book is a work of non-fiction and is based on a true story. The events are portrayed to the best of the author's memory.

Library of Congress Control Number: 2022902244

ISBN 978-0-578-36860-3 Paperback Edition

Printed in the United States of America

xx-v9

Foreword

Our first interaction with Kennedy was via a letter my wife and I received through Compassion International. A simple photograph and sweet few paragraphs written at the hands of a 7 year old living in the Nairobi slum of Mathare, Kenya. Little did I know that a few letters and photos from my wife and I would have a profound impact on Kennedy's life.

My interactions with Kennedy began when I was an USAF officer. I had traveled the world and experienced diverse cultures and their various degrees of freedom. I had hopes, as do most US service members that my contributions would make freedom a possibility for every person I came into contact with. After reading Kennedy's book, I saw how the power of God's grace guided Kennedy to have perseverance to escape imprisonment of poverty. His life story will touch your soul and give you a deep appreciation of Freedom.

Over the years I wondered if our letters and photos really meant anything to Kennedy. Did our monetary contributions make his life better? I was the Doubting Thomas needing to feel the marks of the nails to believe. I never fathomed that a relationship

3

formed solely of letters and pictures with a child would result in a young man reconnecting with me years later via Facebook.

I was overjoyed to hear about and read "This is What Freedom Looks Like", detailing Kennedy's life-long journey and walk with the Lord. Kennedy's book weaves an exciting and transformative account of his trials and tribulations from living in poverty to where he is today. You will learn how the people God put in his path helped him to achieve Freedom and form him into a man of God. When Kennedy speaks of Freedom, he has seen the hard beaten path of hardship but through God's Grace he has overcome and thrived.

I will be forever grateful for the Lord placing Kennedy into our lives and also be forever grateful to everyone who has taken the opportunity to sponsor a child. Kennedy's book will reveal the power a God-filled relationship of letters and photos will make an impact on a child. This book will bring to light how Kennedy utilizes his gifts to help others enjoy Freedom. His remarkable journey will open your eyes to the freedoms many take for granted while cherished and experienced by so few in this world. Share this wonderful book with others so they can see how God can work wonders.

Lieutenant Colonel Darrell Lockhart

Contents

Dedication

This book is dedicated to my kids, Gabriel Baraka and Malkia Grace. I am so honored to be your dad! Nothing in this world has ever brought me closer to God than being your dad, and I have some of dad's wisdom for you. You were released from poverty before you were born. You are the beginning and the end of a cycle. See yourself through God's eyes. Change the world even if you are doing it alone. It does not matter what society thinks of you; it only matters what God thinks of you: BE IT. Never allow anyone to make you feel inferior. Let no one tell you that you can not make your dreams your destiny-they said the same about me but here I am. Impossible is a word that should never exist in your vocabulary. Keep your head up and move forward with confidence. Always support each other, your blood is all you have.

If I could give you three things, they would be: the confidence to know yourself, the strength and courage to chase your dreams, and the ability to always know how deeply you are loved. Do

not ever think you are nothing, and do not ever think you are everything; always know you are something and that you can achieve your dreams.

I love you, my children; never forget that.

Krezi

Introduction

"Let the redeemed of the Lord say so, whom he hath redeemed from the hands of the enemy;" Psalm 107:2 (KJV)

Culture is the customary beliefs, social forms, and material traits of a racial, religious, or social group. (Merriam-Webster) In my view, the cultural upbringing, traditions, and environment that a child is born and bred in shapes how they see, receive, give, and experience life. I see culture as but a system of meaning and shared beliefs. There are many of these systems across the world, some of which are very, not better or worse but, different from one another. The culture of Kenya is one that is very different from the culture of the United States, so when you read this book, try to keep that in mind. However, the differences between our cultures do not have to be obstacles to shared understanding. When cultures interact, they can make positive changes. I hope that as you interact with my culture and experiences, both you and I will have some positive change for ourselves, and the generations after ours, for we owe them a better future.

THIS IS WHAT FREEDOM LOOKS LIKE

I have dedicated my life to be a guardian of freedom, through the United States Army, a children's advocate, through my work with Compassion International (a child-focused, church-based, Christ-centered non-profit) and a Christian, through living and sharing with the world what the Lord has done through me and for me. I also work to spread the hope I have received back into the world through a nonprofit we founded, "Me for My Neighbor," that strives to show the practical love of Jesus by providing food to those in need and supporting small businesses that need a helping hand. By my dedication and work, I hope I can show and give a measure of selflessness to a culture otherwise stricken by selfishness. Through my story, I believe people will learn that there is no sound louder than that of a captive set free.

In this book, I passionately share my personal stories of growing up in the darkness of poverty, pain, hopelessness, sadness, and fear which, over time, God turned into healing, hope, joy, and freedom. To understand my personal stories, you must first understand the "typical" details of where I lived, and what it was like for the "typical" Mathare slum family. There are not very many

available statistics about Mathare, probably because the Kenyan government does not care to know how bad the situation is there. Due to this limitation, many of the statistics about Mathare in this book were paraphrased or pulled outright from the "Mathare Valley Report," a collaborative infrastructure upgrading plan made between Berkeley University, the University of Nairobi, and others. The report was released in December 2011.

Poverty, Pain, Hopelessness, Sadness, Fear

MATHARE

"Life there is a fight to find self-worth and acceptance while living in the lowest economic class of the society. People there live in fear of the governing class, who have no respect for the life of the poor. As someone living in the slum, you are often told that the script of your life was made before you were born. You are not meant to amount to anything."

Nairobi, Kenya happens to host eight slums, with Africa's largest slum, Kibera, being one of them. Mathare, the city's second-largest slum is also the second-largest in Kenya. Mathare "boasts" a population of about half a million people who are packed into roughly 4 square miles. The slum is marked by widespread poverty, prostitution, unemployment, and, naturally, a high crime rate. Throughout its history, Mathare has held a reputation for lawlessness, where economic and politically motivated violence frequently occurs. Most of its inhabitants are very poor and its public infrastructure remains appallingly decrepit. The sensory impact of poverty, the labyrinths of densely packed shacks, the smell of partly open sewage canals, and warnings about the dangers of being exposed to violent crime when entering the area, make strong impressions on any slum outsider.

An aerial view of the Mathare slums. Note the vast expanse of rusty tin roofing sprawling into the distance.

Mathare is not a place you are proud to say you are from, and not the easiest place for children to live and grow up, though many

children live and grow there, as they have nowhere else to go. It is also not an easy place to get an education, as school fees are a luxury many families in Mathare cannot afford, and there are not very many schools either. Despite all the ills that come with living there, many Kenyan families have no option but to call Mathare home. The irony is that around 90% of Mathare's residents are tenants that have no rights.

My son and I visited Mathare in 2017 and honestly – it brought back so many memories!

THIS IS WHAT FREEDOM LOOKS LIKE

A typical family in Mathare consists of 7 members, including parents. The life expectancy of a boy is only sixteen. By 12 years of age, the script states that most boys should already be involved in crime, gang banging, drugs, and its abuses. By 16, most boys should be dead, or close to it, and the script is not that far off. Girls in Mathare become moms usually by the time they are 13. If a mom's first child is also a girl, then by 26 that mom becomes a grandma. If her daughter's first child is a girl, then in another 13 years (or so) grandma becomes great-grandma, and so on.

"G for gun" isn't part of the usual alphabet instructions - this is one of the elementary schools in Mathare.

THIS IS WHAT FREEDOM LOOKS LIKE

A typical family lives in a ten square foot shack made of thatch and dried mud, tin, and even cardboard, with a dirt or concrete floor. There are almost no modern conveniences. For example, only about 10% of Mathare has formal access to electricity. About 10% of Mathare has access to running water inside their shacks. Since Mathare largely has no reliable running water, people either fetch water from local cartels, who illegally tap it from government facilities, or fetch water from either the Nairobi or Getathuru rivers. Page 30 of the report states, "The sanitary infrastructure in Mathare is equally bad and in many cases worse than the water." Toilets are few and far between. People shower late at night, outside under the moonlight, after their neighbors have gone to sleep and use filthy public latrines that clog and overflow regularly. It is not unheard of for one latrine to be shared by 40 shacks or more. Once the latrines are full, young boys are employed to empty them, and those boys usually dump the contents in the river as there are no other suitable places for disposal. It should be no surprise that typhoid and cholera are also serious problems in Mathare. It is nightmarish and dangerous to use the latrines at night as they are also poorly lit. The closest one could be 10 minutes away and thugs and sex offenders are much more active at night. "According to Amnesty International, unsanitary, insecure and poorly lit toilets in Mathare are contributing to rape and sexual violence and fueling the spread of infectious diseases, including HIV." (page 32) Life only gets worse when the rainy season rolls in. The few sewers that exist in Mathare backup much more severely than usual and overflow into the streets and houses that are nearby. With this, residents are regularly awake half the night, cleaning up the human waste that has flooded into their shack. Since most people in Mathare sleep on the ground, a dirt (now mud) floor covered in the shit can be quite a problem, but the day has yet to begin.

In literal terms, Mathare translates to "a difficult or hurried clamber up or over something," which describes life there perfectly, as all those who live there clamber over many obstacles every single day just to survive. Every day is a clamber up and over for the next meal. Even so, it is typical to go 3-5 days without one single meal. It can also be fairly typical for children to die from starvation or

disease after having lived a short life without having anyone who cared about them or loved them.

GOD HAD A DIFFERENT PLAN FOR ME

"For I know the plans I have for you," declares the Lord, "plans to prosper you and not to harm you, plans to give you hope and a future." (Jeremiah 29:11)

I was born Kennedy Okumu, and raised in extreme systemic poverty on the continent of Africa, in the city of Nairobi, Kenya, in one of the most infamous, notorious, and tough slums in the world: Mathare. My society expected me to amount to nothing: to live a worthless life as a weak, poor, and a bad person.

My family and I lived in a 10x10 shack made of tin, wood, and mud with a dirt floor and no windows. My two parents bore ten kids, but 3 of them were dead before I was born. There was only one bed, so my brothers and sisters and I slept on cardboard with wool blankets to try to keep ourselves off of the ground as Mathare is infested with rats and roaches.

THIS IS WHAT FREEDOM LOOKS LIKE

It was normal to be eating our small bits of food while rats chased each other along the walls of our house. We always thought it was funny when the stray cats roaming around would chase and eat them. Occasionally, cockroaches would fall from the roof into our food. When that happened, all we did was just pick them out and throw them onto the ground.

When the rainy season came, everything always got worse. I remember sleeping on cardboard on the floor and sometimes it would rain, and the sewer lines would break and flood our home. My siblings and I would spend the rest of the night getting the nasty-smelly water out of the house. There was no electricity and no running water (except during the rainy season of course), so we used a bucket instead of a bathroom and we cooked outside with charcoal or firewood. We had no furniture (besides the bed), which was just as well because we did not have the room for it anyway.

Despite all of this, my dad never left us and he never gave up on us.

DAD

"Even though my dad had a lot going on, he always was the easiest going person I knew. My dad does not take life too seriously. He is a man that rolled with life's punches."

Since we lived in Nairobi, my dad was considered more economically able than most of his family (even though his only means of transportation was an old, beat-up bicycle). That meant he was obligated to help his brothers and sisters and their families because that is what family is expected to do in Kenya. Due to this fact, we grew up living with our cousins as well. To help us survive, my dad was always working. At one point in time, he was a secondhand clothes tailor, by day, and a security guard, by night, (the security position was owned by an Indian tycoon).

Those two jobs were not the best paying jobs and, as a consequence, the struggle to survive was still very real: every day was a fight. I still remember my dad would hide his pay stubs because he was ashamed of how much he made, but that still did not stop us from finding them. I still can't wrap my mind around how he was the best dad he could be and gave his all every single day while making roughly 72 dollars a month, working 12 hours a day, 20 days a month.

My father's dedication to do his best to provide has spurred me to be a better dad for my kids.

THIS IS WHAT FREEDOM LOOKS LIKE

My dad worked two jobs all my life, my mom made chang'aa and ran a bar to feed the family. Though all that effort, the family was too big that it was still a struggle to feed and raise all of us.

THIS IS WHAT FREEDOM LOOKS LIKE

While he was a security guard, he worked nights, sometimes my dad would come home bruised up from being jumped by thugs. Sometimes they would even steal his old bicycle and, with it, all the money he had been saving for us. I can still recall one day in particular. It was the beginning of a new school year, and my dad had bought us some school supplies while he was at work, and tied them to the bike. When he clocked out from his shift that morning, he went outside and saw 4 gangbangers running off with his bike. He knew he was outnumbered, and he knew he was tired, and yet he still chased them down and fought them; that is just the kind of man my dad is. He came home without his bike that day.

At some point, I do not remember when exactly, he was transferred to guard a fast food restaurant and for about two years, we ate leftover fries and chicken three meals a day, every day. I have since taken a lifetime hiatus from fries and I am not a fan of chicken.

Just so we could survive, dad would bring home stuff that he had picked from the trash, like half broken cups and plates, half a

toothpaste, and old, worn-out shoes. He pulled our baby teeth with pliers and followed through to see us keep our dental hygiene at its best. Sometimes he could not find toothpaste or tooth-brushes so he got us some sticks from an indigenous tree and we used them to clean our teeth. As kids, we thought this was very funny and we still tease him about it to date, but hey, we had to take good care of our teeth somehow, especially since we could not afford a dentist.

My dad was the ultimate hustler. There was nothing he did not give us for survival. Since dad had to work all the time, we did not get to spend much time with him, so we spent time with our mom instead.

MOM

"My mom always told us that we might be poor for now and don't have everything everyone has or what we want but the one thing we had was each other"

Despite having at least seven kids to raise, my mom was the perfect model of the typical hard-working, tough, African woman. Despite the difficulty of her life, she believed in family, meaningful

24

friendships, and community. While my dad was working hard in the city, my mom was working hard at home. She illegally brewed and sold traditional Kenyan liquor called Chang'aa. Chang'aa is 100% alcohol and is essentially Kenyan moonshine. It was stinky and smelly, so it was a practice in our home to smell our cups before drinking out of them. One of the benefits of Chang'aa was that it was an effective disinfectant, so we had a way to clean what dishes we had to combat illness. Whenever we did get sick, our parents would give us a shot of it; we needed only to sneeze once and it cleared our sinuses. One of the drawbacks of Chang'aa was that too much consumption could result in blindness.

My mom was very popular in the area because she loved people, especially children. I remember one time my mom had some kids rescue abandoned a couple of babies floating on a river so she could keep them. I also remember that this pissed off the moms who had them in the river in the first place. Abortion and abandonment was something that happened in the slums frequently.

THIS IS WHAT FREEDOM LOOKS LIKE

My mom made chang'aa (Kenyan moonshine) to raise us. I remember police coming to collect bribe from her every couple days, I remember helping in our little bar to serve adults as a kid. Here's the distilling equipment used to brew the stuff.

THIS IS WHAT FREEDOM LOOKS LIKE

My mom was also a known doula. She helped a lot of mothers who couldn't afford decent maternity services safely deliver babies. This earned her a lot of respect in Mathare and, to this very day, I share my mom with many other people: most people call her mom.

Due to her popularity, mom's brewing business picked up and she became not just a brewer but a local liquor distributor. Since this was an illegal business, it drew the attention of the police. Luckily for us, the Kenyan government, and especially the police, were (and still are) very corrupt. When the police showed up, usually three times a day, they only wanted bribes (usually about USD 2 each time). Since they only wanted money, my mom managed to keep her business alive even though sometimes the police ended up taking all of the money that mom had made that day. That meant we had no money to buy food.

Since my mom was always busy either brewing or serving at the "bar" (our house), she needed us, kids, to help her with distribution, and, sometimes, even serving. I still remember serving adults moonshine as a 5-year-old. We helped out by carrying five-gallon buckets full of alcohol throughout the slum. The streets of Nairobi, and especially Mathare, were, and still are, very tough, so to confuse the many people who would want to steal the moonshine from us, we always carried two buckets, one filled with Chang'aa, and the other filled with water. We also always sent one of our brothers or sisters ahead of us to check if the way was clear of policemen or other thugs.

Even though her business was illegal, and brought about unwanted attention to our family, mom vowed to continue until all of her kids made it to high school. My mom loved her children more than anything. We were (and still very much are) her whole world. When it came to us kids, my mom always believed in us. She always said we would grow into amazing, shining stars. Even though my mom only made it through 4th grade, and my dad only made it through 7th grade, they both highly valued education. They made sure, with the sweat of their brow, that we could, and would, attend school.

They sent me and my brothers and sisters to Karura Primary.

Karura Forest Primary (Elementary School)

"Y'all should not even be in this school!"

- John Okumu Obiero, Principal of Karura Primary

I still have vivid memories from Karura Primary school. It was the closest school offering good quality education that my parents could afford and it was a two-hour walk away from home, in the middle of a forest, just outside of Nairobi.

I remember walking to school, barefoot through that forest.

I remember using the morning dew from the grass as a lotion to hydrate my ashy skin.

I remember wearing my beat-up, hand-me-down school uniform, which was so torn up my shorts showed my butt cheeks.

I remember using a grocery bag for a backpack.

I remember going to school not having had a single meal in the last 72 hours.

I remember doing homework in exchange for food.

I remember begging for food from my school mates when there was no homework

I remember not knowing any life better than this.

29

THIS IS WHAT FREEDOM LOOKS LIKE

In Kenyan schools, we have mandatory morning school assemblies, every first hour on Mondays, Wednesdays, and Fridays. At those assemblies, we hoist our nation's flag together, recite the pledge of allegiance, pray together, and receive announcements from the school principal.

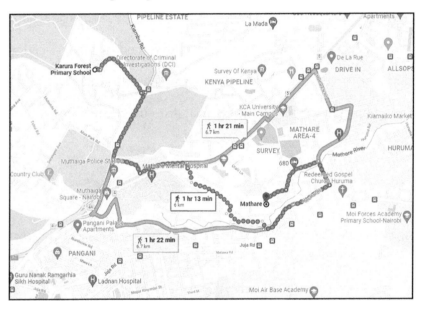

By foot, the journey to school was almost 2 hours daily. Here's an approximate mapping of the distance and time it took from home to school. DATA COURTESY : *Google Maps*

During those announcements, the principal would publicly humiliate students who had outstanding school fee balances by

announcing their parent's names, their names, and how much they owed the school. Those students would then be sent home.

It was always embarrassing for our family; five of us attended the same school and we always had the highest balance. Sometimes the principal would joke by adding that we were not allowed to even be in school. This would mean that we would have to walk the two hours back home from school after just barely getting there.

Despite being extremely poor, my dad always tried to get some cash to send us back to school with. My dad would often give me some of the dresses he sold so I could sell them to get money for school fees. That was how I paid for my first school trip in third grade.

Sometimes we owed about 100 dollars and he would send us back to school with $5, only for us to be sent back home again since the remaining balance was still too high. As kids, we figured that if we were going to be sent home from school for outstanding fees, we would go play soccer at a nearby field instead. This way we did not have to do four two-hour trips in a day to be in school.

THIS IS WHAT FREEDOM LOOKS LIKE

We felt bad about that, though, because we knew our parents would have rather had us in school while they were trying to hustle for the next meal.

Although school could be quite bad sometimes for me, and my siblings, there was one place we went every week that I always enjoyed: church. Mom and Dad were and still are, very religious, and so they made sure we attended as often as our crazy lives would allow, even though they could not always go with us themselves.

When I was a little boy, I always wanted to walk to church with my dad. I still remember the first time I convinced him to take a day off of work and walk to church with me. It is a day I will never forget; that day changed my life completely.

One Sunday, my pastor had requested that we invite our parents to attend church. Even though my dad was always busy, I was able to convince him to come with me. The pastor told the parents about the opportunity to be helped through a public program hosted by a Christian non-profit organization. That day was the first time I came into contact with Compassion

THIS IS WHAT
FREEDOM LOOKS
LIKE

International, through my local church, Redeemed Gospel, in the Mathare area 4A.

ADDITIONS

Since my home was always a bar, I did not go home when my parents wanted me to. When I was 12, my dad told me "if you can't show up when it's your curfew time, just go back to where you have been." I left home then, and I have not lived with my parents since. (you can rent a house at 14, after your rite of passage, circumcision) because you are considered to have transitioned from childhood to adulthood. I lived with my friends then moved in with my older brother Fred then out with friends again.

Life Turns to Compassion

"They helped us go from eating 3 times a week to 3 times a day as a family. They raised me through Compassion International. They gave me hope."

When I was 7, I came into contact with Mr & Mrs. Darrell and Denise Lockhart (USAF) through Compassion International. At that time, they were newlyweds living in Eagle River, Anchorage, Alaska, and they picked up my "sponsor a kid" packet at a Compassion event held in the area.

I remember growing up, I wanted to be like Darrell; I wanted to serve my country and I wanted to be kind. They treated me like I was one of their kids: they always said I had a cute smile. (Isn't that true?)

What do I have to say about them? It is a list of "firsts."

They were the first people to tell me they loved me.

THIS IS WHAT FREEDOM LOOKS LIKE

They were the first people to buy me a birthday gift (who really cares about birthdays in Kenya, anyway? We have real problems like eating).

They were the first to pay for all of my school fees (tuition, books, supplies, uniforms, everything)

They were the first to make sure I went to a library instead of a bar.

They were the first people to tell me I would be great.

They always did their best to make a difference in my life. While their financial assistance was usually all that could be sent, Compassion International enabled them to help me make direct, positive, meaningful changes in my life through mutual correspondence (i.e. letter writing). Communicating with them helped me make decisions that I probably otherwise would not have made.

For example, at age 10, I was introduced to the boy scouts and, with Darrell and Denise's support, I joined as a cub scout.

THIS IS WHAT FREEDOM LOOKS LIKE

History has it that scouting was founded in British East Africa in 1910 and became a member of the world organization of the scout movement in 1964 by Robert Baden Powell and his wife Olave. They both then visited Kenya in 1935 and settled in Nyeri which is located at the foot of Mt Kenya until his death on January 8th, 1941. Since then, Kenya has been a key place where the boy scouts program is deeply run in schools. For the most part, I was the only boy scout who had the required gear for camping because Darrell and Denise always provided these for me. Through elementary school, I earned myself a few proficiency badges and got multiple awards and promotions. I did well enough to be granted the opportunity to be part of the select few who marched past the president on national holidays and, later in the day, have lunch with the president at his official residence, known as the statehouse. I went to a lot of camping activities and engaged in community outreach activities from a very early age.

When I was 14, I had started to go blind. My parents could not afford to pay for the operation. The question was, " should we eat or take care of your eyes?" and so the answer was obvious.

THIS IS WHAT FREEDOM LOOKS LIKE

When the Lockharts found out about this medical condition of mine, they paid for the evaluation and subsequent operation immediately.

They also promised me that if I had good grades in high school, they would pay for my university. Due almost entirely to their support, I started dreaming of a life beyond 16. I started dreaming of a life beyond crime and gangs and drugs.

A life beyond poverty.

A life beyond Mathare.

And I was not the only one; enter Julius.

JULIUS "OTTI"

"We walked home late at night from school, through the forest to the slum, but we knew we were always safe because of Julius and his reputation. My brother was called Julius Otti, I was called Otti Jr."

THIS IS WHAT FREEDOM LOOKS LIKE

My older brother, Julius, is 16 years older than me, though we share the same day and month of birth. He was and still is, a complicated man.

Julius started out living the typical life of a young man in a dangerous slum; He started his life as a gang member. By the time he was a teenager, he had a reputation that preceded him.

My brother was very protective of his family. I remember sometimes my dad would get mugged while on his way to work, and within ten minutes, Julius had found out who had mugged dad and beat him senseless. Julius was also an incredible boxer. I remember, one day, he punched someone in the face so hard it broke the guy's eye socket and his eyeball popped out and hung out of his face.

To my brother, my mom was untouchable. One day, four middle-aged men called her names, and Julius, who was on the other end of the slum at the time, somehow heard about what was happening. My brother made his way across the slum, and when he arrived, he attacked those 4 men in front of everybody.

The incident was reported to the police, but since Julius was a high school kid he got away with it. The police chief said that the details of the incident were unbelievable.

It should also not be a surprise to anyone that my sister's boyfriends were very scared of him, due to his reputation. When they saw him on the street, they would turn and run in the opposite direction out of fear of what Julius might do to them.

Though he was feared by many people in Mathare, a local pastor somehow befriended him and managed to get him to attend church again. A few months later, Julius became a Christian. Due to his prior affiliation with gang life, and probably also due to his incredible reputation, he was able to lead a lot of gang members to the church, and, eventually, they became Christians as well.

After some time went by, Julius got a job as a Sunday school teacher. He even made history as the best summer camp teacher ever. He learned to play the guitar and started to lead worship at church and all summer camps. Everyone looked up to him, including me, especially because he was my big brother.

THIS IS WHAT FREEDOM LOOKS LIKE

Eventually, Julius got a job as one of the teachers with Compassion International at the church, which was a big deal; a lot of missionaries came to our church and Julius served as a liaison. Through his work as a liaison, Julius met a missionary from the USA, Amanda, and fell deeply in love with her. They married, and Julius left Kenya. He moved to the United States to be a loving father of two now, and a great husband; he left Mathare to be a family man. He was 29, I was 13.

At the time, his departure was bittersweet for me. On the one hand, I was very proud that my brother had managed to beat the Mathare script; he went from gang member to church leader, single to happily married, and Mathare to the USA.

On the other hand, his success resulted in his departure from my life at a time when I needed a good role-model that was close to home, though I was not aware of my need at that moment.

I was not aware of how much crazier my life was about to become. I was 2 years from starting high school, and I was childishly

unaware of the rollercoaster drama my life would become at a school called Eastleigh High.

Dramatic High School

"When I was with Compassion Int'l at church, or running around Mathare, I behaved;

I didn't want to become a statistic. At Eastleigh, it was different: I got into a lot of trouble in high school."

NINTH GRADE

At 15, I started attending a high school located in Eastleigh, a more well off suburb than Mathare. Eastleigh, the suburb and the school, is separated from Mathare by a single city street, known as Juja Road. Even so, there were, and still are, many, many people who grew, and still grow, up in Eastleigh and never cross the street to Mathare. They grew (and still grow) up not knowing what happens in Mathare, and what life is like there; they did not want to know (and still probably do not). However, that did not stop the Eastleigh kids from seeing us slum dwellers as just plain different.

THIS IS WHAT FREEDOM LOOKS LIKE

I remember that for lunch we used to eat corn and beans mixed on an aluminum tray. The tray, being metal, would get hot, because the food was hot. Since eating utensils were not provided by the school, I used to bring a spoon from home so I didn't burn my fingers. Eleventh graders would take advantage of me and take my spoon. If I piped up in opposition, I got punched in the face a couple of times. Being from the proverbial hood, I found myself piping up more often than not.

In Kenya, at least at that time, the school was on for 3 months and off for 1 month. After the first 3 months went by, and since I was getting bullied, I started taking boxing classes. I attended boxing in the morning and evening every day for the whole month. When I came back, I had some confidence and I was hot for revenge; I was waiting for the next bully to show up, and, of course, they did. The second week of the 2nd semester, I broke an eleventh grader's nose. The following week, I broke a 12th grader's nose. School days went that way for about a month.

THIS IS WHAT FREEDOM LOOKS LIKE

As that month turned into months, I started becoming more well known at school. I became known as the guy who fights for people who get bullied. Though I was not the biggest person around, I had a personal vendetta against bullies, and that made me fearless. If you got bullied, you would come and tell me about it, then I would find the guy and square him away. I was that guy who fights for other people, and people liked me for my zeal. The unwritten code of Mathare probably helped out too. Part of the hood life in Mathare is that a grudge today is a grudge for life. If I meet you in the streets we are going to pick up where we left off. As it turns out, people didn't want a grudge against me. That defined student to student interactions, in terms of bullies, for the rest of my first year. My mentality at that time was to leave normal people alone; if they did not do anything wrong, then they should be left alone.

There were a few (10-15) other people who were like me, from the Nairobi slums. Some were from Mathare, and others were from other slums, like Kibera. My childhood friend and neighbor, Cyrus was one of them. While he went to a different elementary school than I did we still saw each other after school and at soccer tournaments. Due to our upbringing, Cyrus, I, and the rest of the slum kids had many of the same opinions about school, in particular, and Eastleigh, in general. Naturally, we formed a kind of clique (I would not call it a gang) fairly early in the school year. We fought for each other. If one of us was hurt by someone, then all of us were hurt by that someone. Over time, we started being known in school as a clique. Along with that, we also started becoming more influential at school, and the teachers did not like that one bit.

In Kenya, students occasionally go on strike if their grievances with the school are not met. Sometimes, if their grievances are not addressed satisfactorily, the students set the school on fire. Due to this phenomenon, and our upbringing, our clique ended up on the radar of the school teachers and the police. To be fair, we also gave them plenty of reasons to intensely scrutinize us. Oddly enough, our group did very well academically, but we were still broke, slumland, idiot kids at the end of the day. As such, our group did some pretty crazy shit in the name of survival.

THIS IS WHAT FREEDOM LOOKS LIKE

I remember that we started stealing calculators and textbooks and selling them to other students. I remember we once broke into the school gym, stole a bunch of sports equipment, and sold the equipment to school vendors and second-hand merchants. I remember I stole quite a number of those aluminum trays from school and sold them as scrap. Every day, I would take a tray, some days I took a couple of trays. In a month, I would have gathered 30, or so, and sold them for scrap. 30 trays had enough weight to be worth the trip to the scrap buyer. Even so, I was still broke; all the money I made went to food. After all, I was hungry all of the time, rent, because I did not live with my mom and dad, and school supplies, every once in a while I tried to be responsible, even though I did not like school at all. We, unfortunately, did not limit ourselves to just stealing, as we were also pretty rough around the edges.

I remember that, for whatever reason, our clique hated people who smoked outside of designated smoking areas. Due to that hate, we had a contest, at some point, to knock out the most street smokers in a semester. To do the deed, we would walk up behind

them and hit them hard in the back of the head. I do not remember what we gave the winner.

I still remember another example of this roughness clearly. It had to do with my good friend Cyrus.

Cyrus looked very similar to me. We were about the same build, same height, and weight, and from the back, you might mistake him for me or visa-versa. We shared other similarities too: we did not like being in school, we usually had some sort of odd job in Mathare lined up in the place of school, and we were in trouble 24/7. We worked to get pocket money because we loved having our own money. Whenever we had work lined up, we would check in at school, and then immediately leave through the back. Then we hopped the wall and went home; the school had (and still has) a 5 or 6-foot tall concrete perimeter wall. On one of those days, I jumped the wall alone but the teachers who saw me thought I was him. An altercation occurred and he ended up getting suspended, and later expelled, from school. There was a teacher who insisted that the person who jumped the wall was him, and he got angry,

punched the teacher in the face, and then called the teacher all sorts of names. Yes, some people in our clique were so rough, they even beat on teachers. Unsurprisingly, we spent many a night at the local police station. I never told mom and dad, as they only saw me when I wanted them to see me.

Ironically, or maybe even hypocritically, I was a completely different person outside of school. I still went to church every Sunday, I still exchanged letters with Mr. and Mrs. Lockhart, and I still was a member of the Boy Scouts. During this time, I was even enrolled in a special Boy Scout program called the president's award program. In Britain, it is known as the Duke of Edinburgh's Award, or the international award.

The 2 different people I had become had already started to pull me in opposite directions. As someone who was living in extreme poverty, I was often told by people that my life was pre-scripted before I was born. Growing up in the slum, I heard this script try to dictate what I should look like, act like, dress like, and, ultimately, what I should amount to. That script made the rest of

the society stereotype me because most kids from the slum end up just like the script states. I had to overdress, to compensate for being from the slum. I had to tell people in public that I was from another place, the nearest rich neighborhood, instead of from the slum. I was always ready to fight anyone who brought up that I was from the slum. This stereotype had created the identity crises I went through: the 2 different people that I had become, but that was not apparent to me at the time, and so it went on.

That was only 9th grade.

TENTH GRADE

In 10th grade, I had more confidence than ever as I had lived through a year of breaking bullies' noses. While at that point every other problem child knew not to mess with me or my clique, I still had to play the tough guy. I had built a reputation, and now I had to uphold it. I still remember one day in particular: the day I was shot by a stray bullet by the cops.

I recall that I was walking home from school that day and I saw an old friend of Julius, so I stopped to talk to him. As we

conversed, we heard gunshots. Since we did not know what was going on, we parted ways hastily and I continued walking home. I think I may have walked a block, and a random passerby said, "You've been shot! You are bleeding!" I did not feel the wound until I looked down and saw it. Blood was gushing from a hefty cut on the side of my lower abdomen.

The bullet itself did not hit me straight on, it hit me at an angle. Due to that angle, instead of burying itself in my intestines, which could have been lethal, the bullet grazed me and just sliced me a little bit. Since I did not feel like the wound was life-threatening (luckily it was not) I changed my travel directly to the nearest pharmacy. Since in Kenya a prescription is not required to get any sort of medicine (at least at that time), I walked in and said, "Hey, I have a wound, can you give me medicine?" The pharmacist gave me some powdery stuff and told me to put it on the wound when I got home. The rest of the day itself was uneventful. The wound was very itchy and with a burning sensation. It hurt so bad for the rest of the night.

THIS IS WHAT FREEDOM LOOKS LIKE

When I went to school the next day, I did not mention what had happened; I didn't talk about it until I could show the scar to people. Essentially, I milked the whole event for "street cred." People asked me a lot of questions: "How'd you take it?" - "I just walked home." - "What did you do after you got shot?" - "I went to the pharmacy and got some stuff." - "What about the next day?" - "I came back to school the next day."

I played the whole situation off because I figured other students, and even teachers, would give me more respect due to how I handled it, and I was right. At that time, I did just about anything for reputation. That reputation and street credit, though, did not always garner me the right sort of attention.

In 10th grade, students got to pick their classes, and one of the classes I chose was Arabic. I had always wanted to learn Arabic; to me, the language sounded beautiful. To learn the language, I knew I had to speak it, so I started talking to, and hanging around, Muslim students. I even started to visit the local mosque. I started to get a lot of attention from them, but since I was so well known,

and pretty much friends with everybody (minus those with broken noses and smokers), I did not think much of it at first.

However, at some point, I felt like I was being targeted by Muslim students.

They bought me gifts, a lot of gifts, and it was obvious that they favored me. My guess was they thought that if they got me to convert my religion from Christianity to Islam, they would probably pull in a lot of other people as converts too. The whole situation felt off, and it just did not work for me. I wanted to keep my faith, so I dropped the class, and cut my ties with the mosque. If this created any sort of friction between me and the Muslim population at the school, then I did not know about it.

That last memory reminded me of another concerning Muslim student that did not end nearly as well. I remember that there was a Muslim versus Christian football (soccer) game and that there was an altercation. There was a disagreement about a call or something along those lines, and one of the Muslim competitors punched a good friend of mine in the face so hard his eye started

to bleed. Recall one of our clique tenants: an attack on one is an attack on all. A few weeks later, we cornered him in the school assembly hall and jumped him. He ran through the glass windows, shattering the glass, and went to the school staff room, thinking that it would serve as an asylum. It did not, and by the time we had left, the guy had lost more than just the weeks past soccer game, and the teachers had lost more than just their nerve.

While my reputation made school life easier for me from a physical perspective, that status also brought attention to me that necessarily exacerbated my inner identity conflict. For example, despite my ridiculous antics with my clique-mates, I found myself attaining leadership positions, both inside and outside of the school.

Interestingly, I became a classroom representative (a student leader) that year. Our school principal believed in the old proverb "set a thief to catch a thief," so he made me our class rep with the expectation that I would stop other students from leaving the school whenever they wanted to leave. I did not like that job

because, while I had little respect for school authority, I understood why the students were leaving in the first place. I understood why Nairobi kids, and probable kids in general, have no love for school. School sucks, and they have issues that they have to deal with at home. Due to my understanding, I decided to never report anyone. Other students would even tell me that they were going to be gone one day or another, and I would say, "just don't get caught." I was also promoted into a leadership position within the Scouts that year.

Those leadership positions also helped my reputation with some of the school teachers a little, despite the damage I had done with my friends. What helped, though, was my performance in the drama, which happened to be one of the other classes I chose. That is also when my school popularity took off.

In high school, we had art, science, and music festival competitions, and I shined in drama. When I took my school nearly to the national level of competition, I started to gain favor with some of the teachers, like Mrs. Mwaura and Mr. Omar. I

remember that they would keep me in school when my school fees were not paid, and they would buy me lunch and even hide me in their office. Mr. and Mrs. Lockhart always paid my school fees, but whether they were processed in time for the due date or not was a different story. At that time, international payment processing in Kenya took time, and the time required always seemed to change. Those teachers took care of me in the interim. They also did not want me to leave because they wanted me to practice. At some point in the school year, I started consistently getting recognition, awards, and certificates from the government for my performances. Additionally, I started going to functions in other schools and performing. I even started getting invited to host events, so I knew from that point that I had a special knack for entertainment.

ELEVENTH GRADE

In 11th grade, our clique shenanigans grew to be more encompassing, partially due to our confidence, but more due to our growing, and more importantly looking, older. During this time, I grew a beard and somehow, probably because I looked old enough, acquired an ID that said I was 22. Since we passed for

older than we really were, and we knew most of the bouncers, we started going out on the town.

We never paid for the bus. We always threatened the bus conductors, and even beat them, if they insisted on charging us for the bus fare. Some conductors would report us to the police and come to school looking for us the next day. To escape notice, we either skipped school entirely or just got a new haircut. I remember one time we were riding the bus to town and we were not so lucky: the bus conductor recognized us. He refused to let us get off the bus at our terminus. Instead, he took us to the end of the route and a few other bus conductors were waiting there for us; we got the beating of our lives.

While out on the town, we pickpocketed people we passed in the streets. We mugged and beat people from other slums, like Kibera and Githurai. I still have a scar from when I was caught once in the wrong corner at the wrong spot with people from another slum. They stabbed me in the abs and I bled profusely the whole run home.

THIS IS WHAT FREEDOM LOOKS LIKE

We were troublemakers, that was for sure. Some of my high school buddies got themselves arrested and never graduated. Some others were even shot and killed.

I still remember that one of our group got caught by police one Sunday in the streets and got shot in the hand. He was the most popular guy in the school the next day. I still talk to him; he serves in the Kenyan army now.

Our craziness also spilled over into school, more so than last year, though it was obvious to us that the school was a little more ready for us, to a degree. Eastleigh had a disciplinary committee, and since corporal punishment was the prevailing discipline ideology, the school principal insured that the committee was made exclusively of very tough, male teachers. The thought was that the teachers were so fit and intimidating that they would scare us knuckleheads, though we were not the only ones in mind, from getting rough with any of the teachers. Ideally, the only option left was for us to abide by the school rules. Did that happen though? HECK NO!

We still found plenty of reasons to end up in a room with five big men armed with horsewhips who were ready to knock the crap out of us. We did not get time outs in school, we did not even get spankings; we were beat up.

Me (right) accepting the President's Award from Prince Edward and the sitting president (Prince Edward's left)

I remember my physics teacher, Mr. Kamau, who was also the designated discipline master, once slapped my face with a machete. I dropped that class the same day, though I was very good at the subject. I simply did not trust him anymore. Later on, during the

holidays, I saw him in a bar and I planned on attacking him with some of my buddies, but luckily for him, or maybe us, he left before we were ready to corner him.

For all these misgivings, I did not hate school completely, and I did not hate all the teachers either. I remember that history was always my favorite class in school, even when I was in Karura. As it turned out, in high school, my favorite teacher was also my history teacher, Mrs. Mwaura. She made the classroom feel homely. Though she was so motherly sometimes, she could still switch to teacher mode when we were in trouble. She was known throughout the school to make us do the "Duck Walk" across the school's soccer field as punishment. It was painful in the heat of midday, but for the most part, we deserved it for being knuckleheads.

Like I mentioned previously, though, I was a different person outside of school. As when I was in 10th grade, I still went to church. I still attended all Compassion International programs. I still corresponded with the Lockharts, though I most certainly did not tell them about everything I was doing. I even won the President's Award through the boy scouts. The Duke of Edinburgh's International Award, aka the President's Award, is a non-formal education and learning framework operating in more than 130 countries and territories around the world, through which young people's achievements outside of academia are recognized and celebrated. In this program, I was awarded a president's gold award, and I was given the award both by the Earl of Wessex himself, Prince Edward, and the sitting president of the Democratic Republic of Kenya, H.E President Mwai Kibaki, who is also the third president of Kenya. After completing the award program, I was promoted to one of their favorite assessors, and I mentored the next generation of awardees. Being from Mathare, that was a pretty big deal.

TWELFTH GRADE

At 12th grade, students usually get back to focusing on school because how well you test determines your normal job opportunities for the rest of your life. The Kenyan education system is known as the 8-4-4 system(8 years of elementary school,4 years of high school, and 4 years of college), and the only truly important period of time in the system is the test period in the end. Essentially, you take a one month examination period at the end of the last year of high school where you are tested on everything you were supposed to learn, or supposedly taught. If you score at the collegiate level, then you are set to move on to university. Otherwise, you will have to take bridging courses in order to qualify for admittance, and those bridging courses cost money. If you or your parents cannot afford to send you through those courses, you are doomed to reenter the cycle of poverty. My biggest grievance with the system is that the government took away most of the trade classes, like welding, carpentry, etc. They, in essence, took away the only other way to go, in terms of school direction. I consider the entire system to be a hoax; I find it very unfair.

Due to the emphasis that is placed on the last grade of high school, it is typically the year when all the knuckleheads start to act like good students: No skipping school nor missing class, no arguing with teachers, not much clubbing, and also no girls. All the fun and games come to a pause. During this time, many students

even reconcile with God and start attending religious sessions because the year ends up being very stressful and depressing.

That year was not any different for me. I was the most focused I had ever been throughout my entire school years. I was still a boy scout leader and I was still representing my school in national competitions. I was even more excited about my performances that year because I knew that this was the last time. Despite all that I knew in the back of my mind that I had to get good grades to have a good future and, hopefully, get free from poverty. I stayed late at night trying to catch up on content from 9th to 11th grade. I stayed extra hours at school just to read. During those long hours, the school principal was even kind enough to offer dinner at school. The school was safer for the rest of the students too, since we were all busy studying.

That year was not stressful or depressing just because of school though; It was also the one and only time I ever saw my strong man dad cry.

THIS IS WHAT FREEDOM LOOKS LIKE

One normal day, when I was 18, I was walking home from a Compassion International Saturday program. Thinking back on that day, I even recall that I had moved a mountain of rice and beans just before I left. While on my way home, I saw smoke in the direction I was heading, so I picked up my pace. Fires are common in the slums, and it's not like we have a robust fire prevention/control system, so it is up to everyone who is around to get on-site and help put the fire out, or it will spread quickly. The closer I got to what was most certainly a raging fire, the closer I got to home. When I finally got there, I saw that my home was one of 100 homes that had burned down. We lost all that we had worked so hard for, and it is not like we had much, and it crushed my dad. He who worked his whole life and sacrificed so much for us without a single complaint had reached his breaking point. When I saw him shed those tears, it wrecked me, broke me into pieces. I resolved then and there to be a better person, for my parent's sake. My mom and dad used to tell us growing up that we don't have too much, and all you have is each other. That helped, but not right away.

THIS IS WHAT FREEDOM LOOKS LIKE

After our house was consumed by the fire, I went to live with my high school buddy Denis. His family was more well off than ours, but still, I wouldn't call them rich. They shared all they had with me and accommodated me during my stay. His parents welcomed me like I was their own. He even bought me my first shirt after our house fire. I remember that Dennis was very short-sighted and couldn't see the classroom board, so he often copied my notes. He was and still is, one of the most loyal friends I've ever had. To make money after the fire, Dennis and I sold water in a couple of places, called Majengo and Machakos, every night after school. These places were notorious for not having accessible water. He believed in me and made his family believe in me as well. I am still really good friends with him and that will be there forever. I still get very emotional talking about this. I lived with this family until the Lockharts helped my family and I get a new residence.

Towards the end of high school, my double identity crisis finally came to the center of my mind, and I decided which way I would go. I didn't want to be in trouble anymore, and I was scared that if I didn't get good grades, I would disappoint Mr.

THIS IS WHAT FREEDOM LOOKS LIKE

& Mrs. Darrell and Denise Lockhart, my parents, Compassion International, and anyone who had believed in me up to then. I started to enjoy being in school more, studying more, and I also started making better choices. I kept the faith and my hope alive.

At the end of the year, the finals came and I did fairly well. Passing the tests was such a milestone to cross; even though I had some teachers who believed in me, there were some that passionately hated me, and thought very low of me. There were teachers who had told me that there was no way on earth that I was going to complete high school. They'd prophesied to me that my future was doomed and that I was going to equate to nothing. Essentially, they applied the Mathare script to me. Even though I was a total knucklehead, some of the words coming from teachers, or rather people, I should be looking up to as mentors did not inspire me to be better. I admit that I had made a lot of wrong choices, but still, I deserved better. On the day I did my last paper, I bitterly walked back to some of the teachers who did not believe in me. One specific teacher, Mrs. Ng'ang"a, was always angry and

in a bad mood, from my point of view. Anytime she had come across me in the school hallways, she would say something mean. If she had a stick in her hands, she would hit me with it. I guess my face wasn't something her eyes enjoyed. That day, I dropped my tough kid personality, and I confronted her on a human level. I explained to her that all the words she had told me during my high school really had a NEGATIVE impact on me, broke my soul to pieces, and that were it not for God's grace, I really wouldn't have made it this far. I told her that the curses she had spoken on me were deleted from my life by God and that I was going to have a good story because God is the one who is the author of my faith and life from the beginning to the end. Of course, she gave me a look and an attitude. A tear dropped down my cheeks and like a typical knucklehead, and out of anger, I slammed her table and dumped all my books and testing gear I had on my head on her table and left. I got my closure and that was the end of my high school drama.

Healing, Hope, Joy, Freedom

Mr. Obunga, my friend and colleague's dad, would always advise me on life teachings. There was one specific statement he made that changed my entire life. He said, "Now you are grown up and you are in charge of your life. The world has tons of opportunities presented to everyone. Whether you grew up poor or rich, you are in the same race as everyone else in this world. So, it's up to you to either have self-pity on yourself or make a good life for yourself." These words still ring in my head very fresh. These words changed me.

AFTER EASTLEIGH HIGH SCHOOL

After high school, I completely reformed myself and gained some focus in life. I wanted one determined and dedicated life, not two confused, misdirected ones. I stopped hanging with the wrong group of people, and, instead, passionately pursued any opportunity to leave Mathare. In a common Kenyan setting, you are considered an adult by the culture after circumcision at fourteen, but the government considers you an adult at eighteen.

THIS IS WHAT FREEDOM LOOKS LIKE

It was time to adult up and make my momma proud. From that time on, I took every presented opportunity very seriously. If an opportunity did not present itself, or knock at my door so to speak, I built another door and knocked on it myself. I wanted to move to other places and see what life looked like out there.

At 19, I wrote a departure letter to Mr. & Mrs. Darrell and Denise Lockhart. A letter of departure, as far as Compassion International is concerned, is a formal end of support. For me, that letter represented taking my life onto my own two shoulders. I thanked them for supporting me and giving me a chance at life, for believing in me when I needed that the most, and I also told them that I wished I would meet them someday so I could share my appreciation with them in person. To me, I owed, and I still owe, them a debt that I cannot repay.

I got my first legit job at a book warehouse. We worked ten hours a day, six days a week, and only made USD 70 for the month. That was just enough for me, as a single, college-age kid with not many responsibilities, to pay for rent, food most of the time, and, thanks to God, I would still have some extra money to send to my parents. I remember that I would hop on the hitch of moving trucks on the highway for free transportation. It is pretty common for people in Kenya to do, and most of the time, the hitch-rider would just get off when they got to where they were going. However, some people would get in the truck bed and steal whatever they found. To address this, truck drivers would, upon noticing the hitch-rider, accelerate and then slam on their brakes. The rider would then fall into the bed and the driver would come with a whip or a walking stick and beat them. That happened to me sometimes. It really pissed me off until I figured out why they were doing it.

The working conditions at the warehouse were not great. The bosses were very hostile and verbally abusive and there was also no lunch break. I remember that for dinner, because I still could not afford to eat sometimes, I would go to a friend's house and hang out until late in the night. That way they would share their dinner with me. I knew I wouldn't last at the warehouse: I hated the smell of books and I just hated books period. Ironically, I ended up

writing one. I just hope when they are in a warehouse they don't cause trauma for someone else.

I started pursuing my musical skill and started getting connected with people in the Kenyan music industry. I went to sing at local churches, crusades, concerts; I took my faith very seriously. I recorded songs in local recording studios. I did anything to make money to put in music. That made me happy and proud.

Later in my 19th year, music started paying off a little, and, through God's grace, I was able to achieve my lifelong dream of moving out of the slums. I managed to move out of Mathare into a suburb called Umoja, and my brother, Fred, moved in with me as well. The house I had in Umoja was my first house with running water and indoor plumbing. It was one bedroomed apartment, and I used propane to cook instead of kerosene or charcoal. I was introduced to a very strange new world: Electricity in the house, a balcony, security, basic sanitation, a new culture, and new thinking. This was a culture shock for me. I did not have to worry about being mugged when I walked down the street, not like I was prey

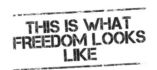

anyway. Neither did I have to worry about the extreme police brutality that went on in Mathare. It was one of my first great achievements and I felt free. In addition, my family and peers were all very happy for my accomplishment; getting out of Mathare, when you start at the very bottom, is no easy, or common, feat. At that point, I had to adjust to a lot of new things. I had to fit in with the new social status I was in, and I also had some financial freedom. I could afford the bus fare, new clothing, lotion, and even cologne, and of course a lot of shoes.

When I finished high school, my parents were of retirement age and they were also empty nesters. My dad retired from his normal jobs, though he never stopped working, and my mom quit her bar and brewing business, since she had succeeded in getting us all through highschool. In the Kenyan culture, when parents retire, they go back to live in the ancestral land and their kids get the responsibility of taking care of them, since we do not have a very reliable social security system. Thankfully, my dad was one of the lucky ones, and managed to draw his social security. I laughed when he showed me that his entire social security, for all the years

he worked, was USD 2,000, and he was very proud of himself: that was the first and only time in his entire life that he had ever had such an amount of cash.

They should have had some inheritance from their parents as well, especially land, but my dad received nothing. My dad came from a very huge family. His dad had 5 wives with a lot of kids. To date, I still do not know most of my relatives. Every time I show up to visit my parents, there is always someone new who introduces himself as an uncle, cousin, or relative that I have never met. My grandpa died in 1998, when my dad was very young, and there were just too many people needing to share the inheritance. Him, being his quiet self, didn't want to be a part of the skirmishes, so he got nothing. I am very proud of my dad for taking a step back in the inheritance part of the deal. In a typical African setting, siblings sometimes play dirty to get inheritance to the point they murder each other.

HANNAH'S VISIT

Ten years ago, my friend, now wife, had just graduated from college, and had always had a desire to go to Africa. She planned to fulfill this desire via a mission trip with a local church, and, as it happened, she knew my sister in law, Amanda, through a mutual friend. After talking to her a bit about Kenya, and what to expect, Amanda and Julius told her about me and said she could contact me in case she needed anything while she was there. In addition, she started babysitting my two nieces (Julius and Amanda's daughters), Olivia and Sami, for extra money for the trip. I have always loved my nieces, and so, despite living so far away, I still tried to have a relationship with them by talking to them whenever I could. Since I talked to them on a regular basis, I also started talking to Hannah. I sent her a friend request on Facebook and she accepted. We began messaging and, quite quickly, we grew fond of each other. The relationship between us grew to the point that we would talk about things strangers who had never met each other would not talk about. The connection deepened over this time due to the hours we'd spend messaging back and forth.

THIS IS WHAT FREEDOM LOOKS LIKE

By the time her mission trip to Kenya arrived, we already had become friends.

She visited Kenya in 2010 with her mom for a month and I met her, in person, for the first time at the airport and the connection and the bond between us got stronger and we grew even more fond of each other. Believe it or not, our first kiss was outside the international terminal at the airport in Nairobi. She then traveled to another part of the country to meet with a pastor

connection she had. A few days later I joined her up there to hang out and meet with the pastor as well. Hannah and her mother then came back to Nairobi.

Around this time, there were a lot of firsts. I took her on a date at a coffee shop in downtown Nairobi. That was the first time I had ever been to a coffee shop.

I had my first pizza during her first visit to Kenya. I introduced a girl, Hannah of course, to my mom for the first time.

THIS IS WHAT FREEDOM LOOKS LIKE

During the introduction, Hannah and Kim made me hug my mom for the first time.

There were quite a few firsts for Hannah as well. She was a minority for the first time in her life. I gave them a tour of the slum and showed them my history. During the tour, Hannah saw, for the first time, people dumping their trash in the street because there was no other place to put it. It was also her first time interacting with orphans. While we travelled, she saw, for the first time, baboons on the road.

She experienced a Kenyan church and got to see a different way of worship. I tell you, in America we sing worship songs, but in Kenya we praise.

Hannah's mom, Kim, also got to experience a culture shock of firsts. As a mom, it was heartbreaking for her to see a little 5-year-old girl taking care of her little 2-year-old sibling because their mom had to go to work to be able to provide a meal in the evening. She said it was her first time seeing someone eating a whole tilapia, including the eyes. It was her first time eating goat.

THIS IS WHAT FREEDOM LOOKS LIKE

Her first time bribing the police (they pulled her over because they knew she would, and could, pay) It was her first time taking public transportation, including the 150CC motorbike. The funniest of them all was that it was the first time she ever saw someone rocking some clean dreadlocks.

One month later, it was time for Hannah, and mom, to go back to the states. The last day at the airport was so difficult. It was the first of the many hard goodbyes. By this time, we knew we loved each other, and would spend the rest of our lives together. We continued our long-distance relationship through Facebook messenger, mail, and skype, even though the internet in Kenya, at that time, was super expensive and unreliable. While Hannah was back in the US, I tried to get a visa to come to visit her but I was denied a visa and that was heartbreaking.

The following year, Hannah came back to Kenya by herself for her year-long medical mission trip. She made a brave commitment to come back for a year to serve at local medical centers. By the time she came back, I was a well-established musician in Kenya,

and I was doing tours all over the country. My music videos and my music were on heavy rotation on local radio and TV stations. She spent her time that year working in clinics and touring Kenya with me. That year was special for many reasons, but one of them, in particular, stands out due to its nature. That year, we decided to attempt to make a difference in the slums of Kenya, and hopefully, the world. We created a movement, and we called it "Me 4 My Neighbor."

ME 4 MY NEIGHBOR

We influenced and started a movement of young people fasting, praying, evangelizing, and raising funds to provide a permanent solution to self-sustainability in slums throughout the world.

During Hannah's second trip to Kenya, I took her on a tour to see Mathare. After a long day spent meeting my childhood friends and seeing where and what I had come from, the spirit of God stirred in both of our hearts. A few months later, some of her friends from Colorado came to visit her and we all went on another Mathare tour and the spirit of God hit us harder. A day after, we were sitting at a coffee shop and we started talking about what we had experienced. We could not stop talking about what we had seen together and we started dreaming of possible solutions. Desires and passions started flowing from our hearts, and it was there, in that moment, that we decided to create an organization to establish hope through serving people living in slums all over the world, through the love of Jesus Christ.

We called the organization **Me 4 My Neighbor.**

THIS IS WHAT FREEDOM LOOKS LIKE

Our mission statement: we are determined to end the vicious cycle of poverty in the slums by addessing the factors that inevitably lead to the high levels of drug abuse, prostitution, and crime found there. Those factors include high levels of illiteracy, the lack of skills, the lack of basic needs such as food, and the lack of mentorship for the younger generation. Our End State: to convert the world's slums into christ-centered market places.

To accomplish our mission, Me 4 My Neighbor (M4MN), in promotion of the gospel of Jesus, works to initiate, facilitate, and manage programs that empower people living in the slums to be self-reliant. The programs provide training, mentoring and a platform to convert their skills into income-generation. At M4MN, we believe in a Hand Up, not a Handout. We started off by skipping one meal a week and spending that money on food supplies for select families in the slums of Kenya in our bi-monthly outreach visits, as we share the love of Jesus Christ. For $26 dollars, we get to feed a family averaging five members for one month. We do this both to help families in need and to begin a relationship

with the members of the community, before we introduce them to the other programs in the organization.

Me 4 My Neighbor programs are designed to be self-sustaining. As much as the organization receives support from friends and partners, we create opportunities to generate resources for subsequent visits, and support the families we visit not just with foodstuff to last a month but with an opportunity to earn a living. We achieve this by supporting a family to set up a business, find an opportunity for work, or assist a child to go through school. Families that benefit from these programs can commit to supporting M4MN with part of their time, profit, and proceeds. Some businesses require as little as $200 in capital to set up whilst their proceeds could feed a family of four. An old adage once said, "Give a man a fish and you feed him for a day; teach him how to fish and you feed him for a lifetime." We are moved to teach, and provide opportunities for, our neighbors in the slums how to fish for themselves as we establish hope through the love of Jesus.

THIS IS WHAT FREEDOM LOOKS LIKE

We also run a program called **#PeopleBeforeProfit**. People Before Profit is a M4MN principle rooted in the value of selflessness. Briefly: as a famous Kenyan musician, I was heartbroken by the fact that our local influencers were either unaware of the social problems in our society or they did not want to bother with trying to do anything about them. In response, I felt called to bridge the gap by introducing them to the idea of running outreach programs themselves or partnering with M4MN. The program #PeopleBeforeProfit itself is an outreach effort designed to persuade social icons, corporations, and small businesses to pursue a cause greater than themselves by showing them the benefits, both to themselves and the rest of the community, of providing meaningful learning and development opportunities that render inspiration, insight, and assistance to people in need so that they can remain positive, passionate, and productive. To us, putting people before profit entails reminding ourselves that all people are unique, special beings, and need to be thought of, attended to, and treated accordingly by highlighting their dignity, and involving them in developmental structures and activities in society.

THIS IS WHAT FREEDOM LOOKS LIKE

In 2019, we partnered with City Lights Church in Greeley, Colorado, and introduced an annual two week mission trip to Kenya every summer. We call it the "Neighbor Weeks." They are the best two weeks of summer. The trip brings a team to Kenya whose focus is encountering God and doing the work that He set out for us in *Mark 16:15 ASV, "And He said unto them, "Go ye into all the world, and preach the gospel to the whole creation."*

Once the team arrives in Kenya, they begin with a few days of team building and settling in, and experience a safari. This is followed by a week long, large scale community project in a potentially remote location. Afterward, we head to Nairobi City to serve with our local church partners, lead high school missions, conduct concerts, participate in a door to door outreach in the local slums, and pray for and share the love of Jesus. It is truly amazing what God can accomplish in such a short amount of time especially when He has a wonderful, anointed team to work with.

We are passionate about creating a community of hope through the practical love of Jesus.

Give below to help us help others help themselves and eradicate the culture of dependency.

To find out more about our organization, visit:

www.me4myneighbor.org.

KIDDO AND K-1

In between Hannah's first and second visit, I applied for a visa to visit her while she was back in the states, and I was denied. While I am still not sure why I was denied, they do not tell you why, at the time, I was pretty crushed. I had spent 4 hours at the embassy, and paid good money, a lot of money for me at that point, and it just did not happen. However, I preserved, and figured that maybe my highschool days were more well known to the government then I had thought and that had caused my visa denial.

As I mentioned before, I made due: we used facebook and email to stay in touch, which was not particularly convenient because, in those days, the internet in Kenya was bad - like really bad. But still, no big deal; I had gone through much worse in the

past, and I figured that interacting with the immigration system would get easier, less time consuming and less expensive, as I interacted with it.

I did not know how wrong I was.

Hannah petitioned for a fiance visa for me (aka K-1) after she got back to the states from her year spent working in the clinics. When she left, she was pregnant with our first child, Gabe, and she wanted me, and I wanted me, to be there when the baby was born. Hannah paid a lot of money in the US just for the petition, and I also had to pay a lot of money in Kenya for the interview. Additionally, I had to go to an embassy approved hospital and pay out of pocket for a deluge of immunizations.

The visa process itself took 11 months to process the request before approving it, and I had to wait blindly. Unfortunately, due to that timetable, I wasn't there for the birth in person: the labor was long, I watched the birth over Skype. Now look, it is not the government's fault that Hannah and I decided to make a baby before starting the visa process. However, does the process really

need to take 11 months? For those readers that are unfamiliar, this type of visa grants 90 days, starting from the time you get off the plane, to get married or you get deported. 90 days is essentially 3 months. For every minute I was granted in the US, I spent 2 minutes waiting in Kenya. Still though, not unbearable, just annoying, and so I persevered.

Thankfully, the wedding was easy, at least in comparison to the immigration process. Hannah's family and Julius and Amanda helped us out a lot and we had the wedding about a month after I arrived. After that, the true difficulties began; I was required to apply for a temporary green card, which lasts only 2 years. In addition, it also costs a lot of money, and takes a whole year from start to finish. The biggest problem? It was illegal for me to work. So, there I was, newlywed with a new baby and I couldn't work at all for a year. If my values would have allowed me to work under the table, I would have, but I did not want something to happen, as it would inevitably have come back on my family. During that time, I learned why people do it the wrong way. The process has been made so hard and so costly to do the right way.

THIS IS WHAT FREEDOM LOOKS LIKE

Fortunately, I managed to get, by the grace of the Lord, my employment authorization near the end of the first year. However, I still couldn't drive because I was not allowed to have a license. That did not stop me.

I applied around town, and got a job at a nursing home. At first, I walked, and, after a while, I graduated to a bike. After the weather turned and the snow started coming down, I graduated to a 1998 Mitsubishi Mirage, with 500k miles on it. Since it would not drive through the snow front ways, I had to drive in reverse through the neighborhood. Perhaps if I would have been born in the arctic circle, I would have just braved the snow, but I was born in Kenya: it does not get freezing cold in Kenya. This time the risk was worth it. Eventually, I got my driver's license and my temp green card, though the trouble with the Immigration process was far from over.

One of the biggest issues in the whole system, at least for me, was the inability to start on the next stage of the process before a set amount of time had gone by: I could not apply for permanent residence until 1 ½ years of the 2 year temp card time had elapsed. So, when 6 months were all that remained on my temp card, I started the permanent residence process. My request for permanent residence was still being "processed" by the time 18 months had passed. Yes, my temporary green card had passed expiration for a full year, and still, I did not know if my permanent residence request would be approved.

The most unbearable part of that time for me was that no one could tell me when or why. "It's still being processed." That was the only answer I ever received. Ironically enough, and this would have been really handy to know from the onset, I joined the army before the processing finished, and the army waived the requirement as a "thank you for your service." Unfortunately for my family, I had already paid all the fees for the process and, as such, I did not get a refund.

By the end of the whole ordeal, after I had become a citizen, I was so incredibly happy: happy that I would never have to deal with immigration ever again!

WHAT IS FREEDOM?

"Who would have thought that this nothing of a boy would turn into a man and now he is trying to raise his boy. Making him understand that Jesus Christ is more than a man, born of the spirit and conceived by the holy spirit, and from his sacrificial death we get total Freedom." - Ken Okumu

This is what Freedom looks like!

Lupita Nyongo once said," Your dreams are valid, no matter where you are from."

That right there is what freedom is.

Julius and I have been able to move most of our family out of the slums. In addition, we have supported our siblings monetarily, emotionally, and spiritually, by helping them through school, and, afterward, helping them set up businesses of their own.

THIS IS WHAT FREEDOM LOOKS LIKE

We have also built our parents a retirement ranch home back in the ancestral land. They are now blessed with 21 grandkids, with the oldest one at 23 years.

My wife, Hannah, and I sponsor a girl, through Compassion, from Mathare. She is from the same neighborhood I grew up in. Every couple of years, I visit Kenya and get to see and spend time with her family. When I visited in 2019, I saw, in my opinion, the most adorable thing in the world: I watched my daughter and her walk down the same streets I used to walk together, holding eachothers hands all the while. That was a super special day. Seeing my kids be the hands and feet of Jesus to someone else in need of love and compassion melts my heart. Being on a mission trip in my old Mathare neighborhood, with my wife and kids, making disciples of all nations fills my heart.

Whenever I work with compassion, I always think about the Lockhearts. I hope and pray that the day will come for the Lockharts and I to experience the fruits of the Compassion

full circle of the work Compassion does in the world: to release children from poverty in Jesus' name.

In December 2020, Julius graduated with a law degree and now practices immigration law so that he can help immigrants assimilate and get inducted into the United States the right way, without having to go through all the trouble that he and I had to go through.

Today, I am writing this book as someone who was not born free, but now lives free. I am married, with two kids of my own. I am part of the United States Army Engineering Regiment, and I have been trained in urban search and rescue. When I was a kid, I always said I wanted to be just like Darell and Denise. I ended up starting a biracial family just like theirs. I now serve God, my country, my family, and the people living in abject poverty all over the world.

I now serve God, my country, my family, and the people living in abject poverty all over the world.

THIS IS WHAT FREEDOM LOOKS LIKE

As part of my service, I speak at churches, conferences, and events all over the world as a partner with Compassion International. When I speak, I tell my Freedom story and advocate for other kids who are not free from poverty all over the world.

DIFFERENT KINDS OF FREEDOM

It is therefore safe to say that I found <u>Freedom</u>. People seek all sorts of freedoms, financial, spiritual, and physical freedom, and those kinds of freedoms are also important. Freedom only exists when there is no confusion within yourself.

Spiritual freedom is very important, because without stability within the self, it is impossible to meet the challenges outside of the self. Examples of challenges and confusion within us come in the form of anxiety, depression, and self-hate. You are not free when there are unending conflicts within yourself. Conflicts within suck all the energy from a person and impede them from thinking for themselves.

Another kind of freedom, financial freedom, is also very important. Just think back on where I came from. The Mathare slums host around half a million people, packed into roughly 4 square miles. These people are forced to congregate in the slums because of economic challenges. Most people in Mathare slums live on an income of less than a dollar a day. To the outside world, these people are not free to leave as they do not have the financial freedom to do so.

FREEDOM

The question we all need to ask ourselves is, "Is <u>Freedom</u> out there or right in here?" To me, Freedom is something that exists solely in my mind, it is a concept. We should not seek Freedom outside ourselves, because it is already in us: we just need to find it within. Freedom is a choice, not want, and unless a person allows that mind switch, they will always want and wait for some kind of freedom to come to them from the outside instead of finding it within themselves.

THIS IS WHAT FREEDOM LOOKS LIKE

Here, at the end, I want to share some examples of how finding Freedom plays out in life, so that, hopefully, it is easier to understand and relate to.

Freedom is:

Freedom is being able to access basic human needs like food, shelter, and clothing regardless of your geographical state.

Freedom is not being subject to necessity, it is being able to liberate yourself from necessity.

Freedom is when where you are born does not make you a societal write off.

Freedom is not living your life proving to society that you deserve to be in it.

Freedom is when where you live does not determine whether you live.

Freedom is being able to live regardless of your circumstances.

THIS IS WHAT FREEDOM LOOKS LIKE

Freedom is having reduced chances of experiencing brutality because of your social class.

Freedom is when I am sure I am not a target of the prevailing bureaucratic enforcers.

Freedom is living in bravery; the fact that I can walk in a dark street late at night without fear of being mugged or being brutalized.

Freedom is when your life is not at the stake of societal pressure or government impunity but only dependent on God.

Freedom is being able to access opportunities regardless of your race, gender, sexual orientation, or economic position in society,

Freedom is when being different does not deny you an opportunity to live and does not make you a criminal.

Freedom is when your efforts in your passion, talents, and skills are rewarded despite your history.

Freedom is when the world rewards you for your merit and not for the privileges of your upbringing.

THIS IS WHAT FREEDOM LOOKS LIKE

Freedom is when my efforts at life bear fruits despite living in an oppressive economic system.

Freedom is when you are not a target just because you are "successful."

Freedom is not having anything in life dictate your future.

Freedom is seeing the fulfillment of your being and being capable of making the envisioned self a reality.

Freedom is when you are the author of your own story, but TRUE Freedom is when you let God be the author of your story.

Made in the USA
Coppell, TX
07 May 2022

77538717R10057